THE
UMBILICAL
UNIVERSE

THE
UMBILICAL
UNIVERSE

S HARON
WHITEHILL

COSMOGRAPHIA

ROCHESTER, NY

Published by Cosmographia Books, Rochester, NY

Book and cover design by Nina Alvarez

Cover photo of Sharon Whitehill's three daughters taken by the
poet herself in 1966.

Cover art "exo planets lit by an alien sun" from Adobe Stock.

For permission to reprint portions of this book, or to order a
review copy, contact:

editor@cosmographiabooks.com

ISBN-13: 978-1-7322690-2-6

POEMS

To Dorothy Brooks, for getting me started;

To my WWWs group, which has helped every step of the way—Colleen O'Brien, Roxanne Hanney, Kay Kimball, Peggydawn Moran, Joani Mountain, Nancy Weaver, and Jet Worth-Dugan—for keeping me going.

To Jim, for backing me up;

And, ever and always, to Leslie, Bonnie, and Dawn, just because you are you.

WHAT IS TRUTH?

Someone I know says
she follows the Truth
(with a capital T)
wherever it takes her.

Hasn't she heard
of the blind men
who found the truth
in a texture or shape
introduced to their hands
as a twist of old rope,
a rough wrinkled wall,
a tree trunk, a snake,
a spear, or a fan?

Truth, I believe, is begotten
in billions of brains
and perceived through
the singular lens of the viewer.

Truth is a plural noun.

My Parents' Closet

Wire hangers disturbed
hiss their cold-blooded breath.
Winter wools release
whiff of musk.

In a corner, a hinged
shoeshine stool stands watch
over a cache of brushes,
polishes, rags.

His shoes, buffed
to a shine, are pregnant
with wooden shoe trees.

Her tailored garments,
sassy as sparrows,
fall in line behind
one favored tweed
preening its feathers
of brown brocade.

His business suits,
lightweight to somber,
migrate from winter
to summer locations.

Her high-heeled pumps,
pouched kangaroo babes
in pocket hanger, curve
shapely arms from
their chambers to cool.

His white Arrow shirts,
her Ship 'n Shore blouses,
cellophane-sealed.
stack the shelves
like sliced bread.

Their cardboard inserts
make crayoned horse-heads
attached to the broomsticks
with tails of torn rags
on which a little girl
walks, trots, and canters.

ALL THINGS MAMA

mother of the thin ankles
scent of lipstick and powder
snap of electric red hair
sides upswept in victory rolls

wise mother who taught me
to tame the wolf prowling the nights,
but who succumbed to the void
that devoured her days

empathic mother who stopped me
from stepping on papa ants
who would never come home
to their children and wives

ironic mother who stood me
in front of the mirror to say,
Under these wrinkles I still feel
exactly like you do inside

brainy mother, possessed
of such passion for words
she knew all but the technical terms
in her thumb-battered *Webster's*

witty mother who quipped
to the humorless surgeon,
on viewing her own bloody tissue,
Why, it looks just like its father

unconventional mother who buttered
her radishes, laughed with a snort,
passed her cocktail olive or cherry
each night to my sister and me

forlorn mother who veiled *The Lost Weekend*
behind other books on the shelf
and hid tumblers of bourbon or scotch
in her vanity drawers

cruel mother whose vile night-mouth
spewed pollution and poison powered
by bottles our father poured down the sink
but replaced the next day

gone-to-waste mother, born too soon
for Prozac, too late for Friedan,
her thumbed *Webster's* concave as stair-
treads curved by generations of feet

sweet mother with white peasant blouse
stretched around freckled shoulders
in my dreams, aromatic with powder
and lipstick rather than liquor

THE FOX FARM

I prized her horsey perfection:
mahogany coat with roast-chestnut gleam,
breathed deep of her pungent perfume,
pressed my nose to her velveteen muzzle,
plumbed her eyes with my own, warmed
winter fingers beneath the twin streams
of her breath, relished the tickle of rubbery
lips that so skillfully captured an apple.

> When my father brought horsemeat home
> from the fox farm in ten-gallon tins
> it pained me to see our dogs wolf
> the stringy red lumps. He pointed out
> how I savored lamb chops for dinner,
> even the livers of calves. *One life*
> *to nourish another*, he said.
> *We all have to eat.*

I reclined with my head on her rump,
sat facing her tail, crouched under a belly
as bulbous and tight as an unbaked potato.
Bareback, I clung like the Velcro not yet invented,
hand wrapped in a hank of her mane.

Adolescence diminished my ardor:
her ankles grew swollen from standing
in her stall. My father chafed, threatened
I'll sell that horse back to the stable.
Guilty, relieved, I turned a blind eye,
left her to graze in the pasture,
dozing and dreaming alone.
One day I stopped and stroked her mahogany hide.
She paid me no heed. A swift swish of tail
stung my cheek, but I laid it, still tingling,
against her indifferent neck, took in the intimate
tang of her mane, let my tears soak her rough coat.
I knew I'd betrayed her, couldn't pardon my part
in her premature fate. Months later, a final image:
her pasture, empty.
Still, life feeds on life
and dogs, even foxes,
must eat.

Papa Only Made Omelets

Papa, you chopped me in pieces,
minced me under your knife,
crumbled me into your skillet
like bacon, whipped me up
to a froth. You melted me down
to a sizzle, left me seared,
spitting hot words in your face.
So often I fled from the table
in tears. So often I burned,
and you burned, in separate rooms.

Papa, you beat down my words,
folded in flavors you favored,
and seasoned me strong with essence
of Papa, garnished me with your frown,
then turned me out on your plate
for inspection. I, the daughter
you never ordered, was never
a dish to your taste.

Papa, why did you never allow me
ingredients outside your cupboard?
Why insist I follow your recipe only?
Why not delve to the depths
of the strong yellow onion or peel
back its layers to nurture the germ
at heart level?

Today I'm attuned to the quiche,
fraternize with frittatas, sorrow
with fallen soufflés. I savor the startle
of garlic, dance to the dazzle of basil,
revel in fennel, soar high on a horseradish
hit. Today I picture the omelet as greasy
with ego, coated with cavil, curdled
in choler from too high a heat.

The omelet's our legacy, Papa.
It lives on, as you do,
in me.

THE WAY I SEE HER

One week

A screaming red scrap
no nurture can soothe
bounced hard into crib
by a mother rejected
then wracked with remorse.
Born angry, this baby
arches away from the breast
spits out the nipple.

Two years

A long-drawn first howl
provoked by a tumble
or bump, at the end loses breath:
eyes rolled back, face blue,
helpless against the spasm
until her lungs fill again.
Raw the rest of the day,
primed for another
eruption.

Five years

The night before school
she abandons her blanket,
develops a taste
for hot pepper extract
painted on fingernails
chewed to the quick.

Six years

Pale between black and brown friends
heedless of civil rights violence
nearby in Chicago, she shows off
her Jackson 5 coloring book.
Jackie, Tito, Jermaine, Marlon,
and Michael: which combination
to crayon first? Three little girls
who don't read the headlines:
"Two Die as Police Shoot
it Out with Black Panthers."

Eleven years

All summer she wears
long-sleeved tops to conceal
her arms, deemed too skinny.
That winter she marks
the mechanics and grammar
on college papers for me.

Thirteen years

In my blue bedroom
she sits on the floor,
reads from a book
about goblins and ghosts.
The quirky wit of the author
plumbs deep wells of delight:
our funny-bones match.

Sixteen years

A vile curse aimed at me
spews from her mouth
as we stand on the stairs.
My slap dislodges a cheap gold stud
from an ear newly poked with a needle.
Blood leaks from the lobe,
and I too am pierced.

Seventeen years

She drops out of school,
boasts of drinking her meals,
staggers home, cracks the glass
on a painting I treasure.
A staged intervention,
a counselor amazed that a girl
with an IQ of 183 must apply
for the GED.

Nineteen years

My ill-chosen words for the man
she's determined to marry:
"I'd like to squash him flat
like a bug." When their divorce
overlaps with a loss of my own
we weave together the strands
of our mutual pain like a rope—
a lifeline that after a lifetime
of frayed expectations binds us
together. We cook, commute
to classes, interpret the Tarot,
read Runes, create mandalas
to illustrate ironic insights and jokes.

Twenty-one years

"I was raped last night, Mom."
Too exhausted to move,
defeated and bruised,
she has collapsed in a chair.
A wealthy young man at trial
serves less than a year.

Twenty-three years

She moves to Arizona,
leaves my fridge bare

of bok choy, blue-green algae,
black rice. A forgotten tube
of shampoo shouts *Free Radicals!*
Save your Follicles! In my letter
I cartoon protesters with signs
that demand FREE US!
FREE THE RADICALS!

Twenty-five years

Her degree self-designed:
"transpersonal psychology."
Her artistic gift expressed
in jewelry, handbags, clothing
and tapestries woven of tiny glass orbs
to resemble a delicate chain-mail.

Thirties

Dedication to art requires
hard physical work to survive—
farmer, tree-trimmer, beekeeper.
Labor too taxing to be sustained
surrenders to service and retail.
No promoters, no venues, no sales,
no surprise: all her knowledge
of Plato and Jung, anthroposcopy,
and quantum physics fails

27

to put food on the table.

Forties

Suspicious, cynical, bitter,
she repudiates anti-depressants,
refuses to fly or to vote,
believes controlled demolition
brought down the Twin Towers,
chemtrails drop poison,
a sinister shadow government
stage-manages all.

Fifties

Counter-cultural values matched
to a chronic negative outlook
generate bona fide misanthropy.
"I never wanted to be here,"
she said long ago. It is difficult
not to believe her.

FIRSTBORN

Unguarded, she speaks
in the voice of the child:
Why did you have to go
and have two more babies?
We all laugh. She laughs herself,
at herself. But the little girl's there
in her middle-aged plaint:
Why wasn't I enough?

"Let me tell you about
how it was for me then,"
is what I want to say.

Your pudgy legs at fourteen months
dangled below the crook of my arm
as I carried you off to your crib.
You were my baby. You,
not the infant I'd already carried
almost to term.

Away to give birth, I returned
with the newborn. You, too shy
at first to approach, unaware
how I'd ached for you for a week,
edged closer and closer. Silently,
gently, laid your head down
on my knees.

Later, when I shifted my focus
from you one day, you repeated
the gesture. That time I moved
away from your head, precious head.
Did you sense my claustrophobia?
I fear, to this day, that you did.

Infant howls of pain brought me
running to find the imprint
of your teeth on her tiny fingers—
an outrage that seemed at the time
more persuasive than the trust
I saw on your face as I lifted
your hand and against all advice
bit down hard. Stereophonic
screaming no comfort to any
of us, as I, self-sickened,
contemplated my imprint on you.

My conscious act of betrayal.

Mama's Big Girl, so sweetly
compliant, yet you were sly.
Someone spilled sugar
on my clean floor. Someone
hung off the clothesline,
dragged the wet washing
into the dirt. Years passed
before your siblings convinced me
I'd punished them in your place.

Surrounded by boxes
from yesterday's move,
already halfway through breakfast,
a lightning bolt struck my heart.
Today was your seventh birthday.
Drowned in our floods of *I'm sorry*,
you managed to surface a smile
but I should have known the sadness
you buried that morning
would linger for life.

After my fight with your father
you cried on my neck, afraid
of divorce. In impulsive denial

I uttered a pledge I had no right
to make—again, a betrayal,
the worst. I was jubilant
when we moved from the house,
but you grew quiet, secluded yourself,
made no middle school friends.

Your adolescence hit hard.
You, so attuned to my words,
you who would stop me for hugs
in the hall, now closed your ears
and rejected my touch. Where
did you go? Betrayed in my turn,
I mourned for you almost as if
you had died.

"This is a song about loving
and letting go," said the singer
while I sobbed aloud in the loft
of the choir. "She'll come back,"
other mothers consoled, but you
were so far away, it was hard
to believe.

You did. You came back
and you love me again.

Yet oh how I wish you had known
in both gladness and grief,
oh how I hope you know now:
you were always, always
enough.

YOUNGEST

Delaying, dawdling & dreaming,
would not make your bed,
refused to tidy your room
or help pick up toys.
Such a baby, taunted your sisters.

Singled out for covert persecution
by the sister whose power to persuade
the adults trumped your constant
complaints, you were helpless
until you resorted to guile & stealth.

Starved for savor, for sweetness,
you secretly stole the prized skin
from leftover chicken drumsticks,
feasted on Halloween candy,
but vomited milk I insisted you drink.

Trapped between choosing allegiance
to me or joining your sisters' rebellion,

you suffered banishment with them
to your father's strict household,
your relative innocence disregarded.

Your lack of animus toward me
came clear on your summer trip:
99 Flake ice cream cones in Westminster,
feeding pigeons in Trafalgar Square,
perched on a cannon at Edinburgh Castle.

Transformed before twenty
to trimness by living on grapefruit
for weeks, you lost undesired,
undesirable flesh, though what remained
was too thin a skin to feel safe.

Left behind at a party by your "evil"
sister (a term you employ to this day),
you lost your virginity to a crude boy
& were punished with grounding
for not coming home until morning.

Depressed & abandoned
by first love, you lived for a time
in a sleazy motel, swaddled
in squalor, accompanioned only

by your little black dog.

Home again, you unleashed your pain
at maternal injustice—*She was always
your favorite, I never came first.*
Buttressed by anger, wounded
anew in my attempted tough love.

Aftermath of a painful infection
—white patches of scalp among the waves
of your lovely long hair—you never knew
how the sight seared my heart
with a tenderness I could not utter.

Safely encased in a surplus of flesh
& surrounded by clutter, the needy
child you were is embodied today
in your hungry first-graders, each sustained
by the love you once needed yourself.

LAKE MICHIGAN BLESSING

She was blindfolded in a red kerchief,
guided by Robin on one side, Tanya
the other, but she had faith in her friends
although she walked in darkness.
They had a surprise, they said,
but not for her birthday. They knew
that she was already fourteen.

Alert to the wood-splintered stairs,
she was glad for the tickle and squeak
of the sand when she kicked off
her flip-flops. Still, she was perplexed
when Robin lifted the blindfold
and Tanya reached for her hands,
pressing palm against palm.

"We told you we had a surprise
in case you said no," they confessed.
"Don't be mad. We're scared of you
burning in Hell for not being baptized."

She knew very well
when you died you were dead,
but allowed them to lead her
into the lake, felt cold clasp her ankles,
then knees—no intercession
on her behalf from the sun.
Hands at her waist, on her head.
Dunked.
She bobbed back like an apple.
In the name of the Father
(dunked)
the Son
(dunked)
the Holy Spirit

It was finished. She thanked them
because they cared, had blessed her.
She let them believe they had helped
her believe she was saved. Wiped
the colorless lake from her lashes,
squeezed out her hair, joined
in a three-way embrace that left
them all dripping and shivery.

Skin warmed from above, heart
warmed by their fear for the soul

she didn't believe she possessed,
she mounted the hill, flanked by friends:
three giddy girls linked as one.
She whose salvation they sought
garlanded now by the red kerchief
they'd draped round her head
like a crown.

CONVERSION

candy-bar thief as a child
shoplifter after her teens
smuggled porterhouse steaks
into purse as young wife

because she led a charmed life
she knew nothing could harm her
no matter the depth of the dive
she would resurface unscathed

even caught by the law she escaped
with her tears and her faithless
"God bless you," melted the steely
resistance of the court clerk

she resurfaced unscathed
from the depths of that dive
which confirmed no harm
came to such a charmed life

what broke the spell of the charm
when maturity motherhood
law and morality failed?
one insoluble shock

she looked death in the face
the cold iron no petition can melt
the deeps that no blessing can plumb
and resurfaced converted

Houses

To house, to contain, to cover,
to hold, to protect, to enclose,
to keep safe. After it burned,
Kay said her house had betrayed her
and I understood.

When my feet crunched broken
beer bottles on the front walk,
I chased teenagers out of my bed,
found ashes and cigarette butts
in the tub, the toilet seat cracked,
the wastebasket half-filled
with urine, I felt like my house
had been raped.

Though I'd furnished that house
to comfort and hold, I once
let a merman who sang from the rocks
of desire beguile me. My house and I
weathered both lover and storms,

rebuilt the edifice one painful brick
at a time.

I began in the womb of my mother,
I lived in that room in the house
of my mother, and so did you.
Within your homesteads and havens
and huts, your townhouses, trailers
and tepees and tents, your chalets,
condos, and caves, you have lived
in the house of yourself.

A woman *is* her house,
that's the main thing.

CARPE DIEM

In early September I sit
with our friend and her nephew
while you lie in a coma
oblivious to the crash,
the medics, your hospital bed.
Brain-damaged, adrift
at the edge of non-being.

The three of us sit face to face
on my carpet, gold shag,
drinking red wine from a jug.
I float, a goldfish gasping for air
at the brink. When I speak
about you, my words rise
fish-bubble empty.

You, who never believed
that the god of your guilt
is a fiction—you have been
disappeared. How do I hope

for the life of your body,
beloved, reduced to a no-thing,
an absence enfleshed?

I lament, the nephew listens.
His eyes beneath the dark brows
are unexpectedly kind, his face
so good-looking it startles.
Our good friend, yours and mine,
pours more wine from the jug.
She understands, holds my hand.

I fall under a spell, emotional
shock held at bay by the warmth
of wine, friend, and man, caught
up in a moment quixotic, surreal.
He is drawn to my heartbreak,
I to the hunger for strong
living arms.

False gold discolors. So grief
becomes gloom over time
and no longer appeals. Yet the time
is not wasted: we take, and we get
what we need for the moment,
even if only an image, a shadow
of love.

No magic carpet, this shag.
It is September again and again
the winter will come, I will bear
the unbearable breach, I will watch
as the gap of your absence
firms over as swiftly and surely
as fishermen's holes in the ice.

DENIED GRACE

You stumble in, bent
by a burden of news.
"I've been denied Grace."

No. Not you, my good
Calvinist lover, so certain
of being among the Elect.

"It's true." You pace
the room. Your stare
is inscrutable.

Wild thoughts skitter
like brain-rats: *I* am
the engine that drives
this eternal damnation.

Yet what does it matter—
vehicle, driveshaft, or engine—
if sin is predestined by God?

Your own doctrine damns you.
It is the source of this damning
and damnable scene.

WALKING THE DOGS

The dog warden knocks,
tells me the neighbors
complain that I walk my dogs
"in gangs."

Walking the dogs. The loss
of this small but significant
ritual rankles. I miss exercise
right before bed. I miss
the infusion of seasonal blends:
the menthol of winter, the raw
scent of earthworms in spring,
the summer aroma of grass,
outdoor grills. Each concoction
a tonic.

What harm, I rationalize,
if a paw bends a few blades
of grass? Don't my innocent
canines have equal right
to this world?

So again I watch as they bolt
up the block, joyously drunk
with release. Again tonight
I savor the sweet weedy flavor
of autumn, a potent champagne.
Again the dogs race to the field
where they make their deposits,
then sprint uphill to the woods.
Up here, the wind is rambunctious,
stirs up the stars in a dark bowl
of sky.

Headed home when
a window flies up.
You! Woman!
A rageful man:
I know you, Woman!
I know you, your gang
of dogs!

I hurry past, sink down
on a stoop near the corner,
give way to tears. Even here,
in my town, my haven, my niche,
livid men with lush lawns
hide in their houses and hate.

Hushed, sympathetic, the dogs
press themselves to my knees,
lick my face.

I shake my head. One crabbed
person does not equal "neighbors"
or "livid men." I wish
that instead of slinking away
I had shouted at him:

I know you, Man!
Hear me, Man!
This beautiful world
belongs to us too.

THE SMILE

For all that rakish tilt
of her floppy suede hat
implies sense of humor,
her incessant smile
chews at my temper.
Its beam is undimmed
no matter the message:
My student Jerry
(nodding and smiling)
dragged by a car
(nodding and smiling),
in the hospital now.

Her too-frequent gifts
(recipes, clippings, a flower)
grate on my ungrateful
nerves, while her earnest
responses to ironic gripes
or to my witty rants
(Have you tried…?

It might help to…)
squelch repartee.

She, of course, is fine:
no requests for support,
no complaints, no self-
disclosures to join her
to friends. She's beloved
by her students, blissfully
wed to her soulmate,
a gourmet cook
who's made dinner
for Julia Child.

Oh, that perpetual smile!
I blind myself to its dazzle,
deafen myself to its call:
love me, love me.

That smile stands between us,
estranges, brings out my worst.
Makes me consciously cruel.

BEACH SONG

Blown sand skates on a road
burnished by sodium lights.
We dart between hoods and trunks,
strobed by beam-and-blink lights.
Your arm on my back unforeseen.

We crest the dune, kick off shoes,
skin socks from our feet, abandon
them on the sand—sugar-sand,
singing sand, sand on a beach
leached of heat. The wet-cement
taste of night air combines
with the raw scent of fish.

Moon-flung shards of light
cut the waves, shimmy shoreward,
meet us halfway as we pitch
down the dune, gravity-seized.
Lake wind snatches our breath.
My heart beats in silent arpeggios.

The crush of dried foam under soles
returns me to childhood: the punch
of my pink rubber boots on ice
newly forming on puddles at dusk
but shattered to hasten the spring.

We walk the length of the pier.
You rest your chin on my head,
my cheek presses your chest.
Your heart under my ear thrums
its thunder in counterpoint
to the rhythm of waves.

What looms in the shadows
beyond the red lighthouse?
What roman candle of hope
has the night beach ignited?

The sky is vast. Your shirt
smells like sheets hung
in the sun. We breathe in
and breathe out. Warm
in your arms I feel safe
as a child, safe from the shame
of alone, from the longing
that weeps in the dark.

I take this night into my blood
and my bones, store it against
future darkness.

TALK TO ME

In the great silence of farm
fields where you grew up,
there was no talk at all.
You starved for it, hungered
to fill up that stillness with words
and more words. Nourished
yourself, by yourself, became
spinner and weaver of words
of your own.

But it wasn't enough.
Initiatory talk, the therapist
called it, the kind of talk
you are so greedy for.
Someone who does more
than listen, someone who
talks for you, talks *at* you:
that's what you desire.

So many times you invaded

my reading or writing
or comfortable quiet.
For you, no such richness
as I found in silence, you
so famished and thirsting.
"Talk to me," you insisted.
"Don't read. Talk to me."

But talk-on-demand erased
every thought, brought back
my father's "What shall we
to talk about, Mildred?"
along with my mother's
impatient reply: "No better way
to squelch conversation
than to pose such a question!"

I agree. Good talk
is a ping-pong game,
words bounced back
and forth, your turn,
then mine. "Talk to me"
tips the table.

No ping-pong paddle for her,
your new love. No. She ladled

words on your plate like thick
porridge, poured out the clever
self-mocking cocktails you craved.
That's why you left me: because
I don't talk, *cannot* talk that way.

True to form, you swilled her,
ingested her, took your mortar
and pestle to her imperfections.
Spat them in her face.

The heave of her recoil
upended the banquet,
left you sitting in silence.

THE
UMBILICAL
UNIVERSE

We try to find our way to each other,
my middle daughter and I—my suggestion
that we begin with beliefs. Mine,
that existence is random, that life
has no ultimate meaning but humans
must live *as if* meaning exists.

You despair for the world, Mom,
but I see the breakdown of customs
that hold us in thrall as a positive
transformation, this current regime
only an agent of change. You say
humans must live as *if* meaning exists,
I find meaning in everything everywhere.
How can we grow, come together,
rooted in soil from such different planets?

My *as if*, dear, is not despair. I wake
happy, hug my mate
loving the rasp

of his beard,
prize my dexterous
fingers on the keyboard, relish
the rising bubble of joy that bursts
into laughter with women I love.
I shrink from our new naked
emperor, absent all moral compass,
but I reframe the widening gyre
of the world as a spiral and trust
that good will prevail.

**You and I both want what's moral
and fair, but we'll never agree
what that means. Anger and tears—
we can't talk without them, but still
we have closeness of heart.
You're my mommy and always will be.
If that's the best we can do,
it's not nothing.**

Darling girl, you bring me to tears.
Your soil may be silty, mine sandy,
but this *is* the same planet: the imperfect
planet of mother and daughter, the planet
called love.

MESSAGE TO
MY DAUGHTERS

When you three were small,
my two hands were never enough
to hold all of yours, the image
of failure.

These are my images
of you today:

Leslie, you scrutinize animal life
on a tea-colored Florida creek
as I contemplate rivers of words.
You nurture garden greens, yellows, reds,
walk winter woods as your cat
tags along, invent tasty dishes
nearly too pretty to eat. We connect
via phone, wait for mutual visits
to catch up on physical hugs.

Bonnie, no longer the child,
her blond head agleam, bent to sniff

a red rose, you bloomed into an artist
and searcher, keen to put space
between home and yourself.
Our scraping against one another
thickened your skin, tenderized mine:
your laugh still rings chimes in my heart.

Dawn of the sloe eyes, fetching smile,
freckled nose, you hardly present
as the widow you are. You're immersed
in students who leave you love-notes
and cling to your leg. Engrossed
single mother, reader and thinker,
you're sharp on the uptake
but never not down to earth.
Our sporadic parleys enliven us both,
satisfy like a deep breath.

My daughters, my dearly beloveds,
I send these fresh images to you
with love.

Life's Work

For decades I saw
my most meaningful
task as the search
for a soulmate.

Not so.

For years I toggled:
an angel one minute,
a fishwife the next—
a miner unable to separate
gold from the fool,

while the child exhumed
from my past, weighted
with festering wounds,
infiltrated the troop.
An unwitting commando.

Decades later I recognize

my most meaningful work:
to grapple with the child-in-me
disguised as a mother.

No question, no doubt.

ACKNOWLEDGMENTS

Many thanks to the publications in which these poems previously appeared:

THAT Literary Review, Number Three (2018): "Papa Only Made Omelets"

Chaleur Magazine (2018): "The Way I See Her"

And further thanks to my editor, Nina Alvarez, a great pleasure to work with.

ABOUT THE AUTHOR

A retired professor of English at Grand Valley State University in Allendale, Michigan, Sharon Whitehill now lives and writes in Port Charlotte, Florida. Her publications include two scholarly biographies, *The Life and Work of Mary O'Hara, Author of My Friend Flicka* (Edwin Mellen Press, 1995) and *Frances Gillmor, Aztec and Navajo Folklorist* (Edwin Mellen Press, 2005). Whitehill has also published a children's book, *The Lizard Wizard* (Xlibris, 2003) and two memoirs: *On the Trail of Flicka's Friend* (Fithian Press, 1995) and *Sweet. Bitter.Sweet* (BookBroker Publishers of Florida, 2016).

She lives with her husband of twenty-one years, Jim Meloy, a former beekeeper and jet engine mechanic.

www.ingramcontent.com/pod-product-compliance
Lightning Source LLC
Chambersburg PA
CBHW031947070426
42453CB00007BA/497